Tulika

The Shining Stones

at a Stone Age site in India

by Shanti Pappu

illustrations Ashok Rajagopalan

Dedicated to my family, my colleagues, villagers at Manamedu (the site of Attirampakkam) and to the memory of Robert Bruce Foote who discovered the site in 1863. – SP

The Shining Stones
© *text* Shanti Pappu
© *photographs* Sharma Centre for Heritage Education
© *illustrations* pages 12, 13, 26, 27: Shanti Pappu; rest: Tulika Publishers
First published in India, 2007
ISBN 81-8146-172-X

This book is based on excavations at Attirampakkam, Tamilnadu, India, which form a project of the Sharma Centre for Heritage Education — www.sharmaheritage.com.

Published by
Tulika Publishers, 13 Prithvi Avenue, Abhiramapuram, Chennai 600 018, India
email tulikabooks@vsnl.com   *website* www.tulikabooks.com

Printed and bound by
Sudarsan Graphics, 27 Neelakanta Mehta Street, T. Nagar, Chennai, 600 017, India

For more information about Tulika or to order books visit our website www.tulikabooks.com

Digging up the past – in the classroom

Children are very curious about the origins of things. 'How old is the earth?', 'Why does the elephant have a long trunk?' – are some of the questions parents and teachers may be confronted with.

In school we read about the Mauryas, Satavahanas, Pallavas, Mughals and other great dynasties of the past. Most of us believe that India's history began with the Indus Valley Civilisation. Some textbooks talk of the big stone burials of the Megalithic period; a few touch upon Early Man or the Stone Age. But do we know that stone tool making groups lived here more than a quarter of a million years ago?

Who were the first people to live in India? What did they look like? How long ago did they live here? How do we know that they did live here?

These questions are difficult to answer, and we may even believe they are not relevant to what children learn in school. But think. The very fact that we stand erect, turn the pages of books with our hands, create art, think intelligently (most of the time), make choices, cook food, dance, sing and speak – all these are the result of human evolution beginning in our prehistoric past. Sculptures and monuments carved of stone can be traced back to the first person who chipped stone into tools or weapons.

This book takes us back to the period before written scripts, to prehistory, the Stone Age and *Homo erectus*. It can be used to address questions of how our earliest ancestors lived and adapted to changing environments, for plays and workshops, and to build on themes of the environment and the human body. It also draws children into the archaeological process of uncovering history – of slowly and carefully digging up the past.

– Shanti Pappu

A Most Important Place

Selvi raced across the fields. She did not feel the blazing sun above and burning sands below. She was to carry a new pickaxe from the village to THE SITE. "Run!" said her mother.

THE SITE was a patch of village wasteland — red earth and pebbles. Goats grazed here on spiky thorny bushes.

The whole year round Selvi's little village of peanut farmers, Attirampakkam, lay forgotten, deep in the foothills of the Allikulli hills. Mothers and fathers and aunts and uncles and cousins worked in the fields from morning to night. Selvi went with her brothers and sisters to the village school.

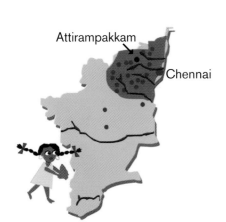

Attirampakkam

Chennai

● Lower and Middle Palaeolithic sites in Tamilnadu

The teacher slept and swatted mosquitoes while the children talked and fought and played in the yard. Selvi loved the pictures in her books and wished she could study more. But her father was very poor. She knew she would soon have to leave school and work in the fields.

Once a year, just before the peanut harvest, the village sprang to life. That is when the archaeologists came — a team of young and old people from all over the world, with maps and books and shining machines. They came to dig ancient tools and weapons now buried in the red soil of the village.

Fathers and uncles sat sharpening pickaxes, knives and spades. Mothers and aunts talked and laughed as they cleaned sieves.

An archaeologist (aar-kee-o-lo-jist) is someone who tries to understand how people lived in the past, by studying things they left behind. I am an archaeologist.

Selvi's grandfather, aged 93, got his whistle cleaned and stick sharpened. He had been the night watchman on the site for the past five years and was not about to give it up in a hurry. Even the goats danced around in the sun.

Selvi gave the pickaxe to her father. Her little brother Selvam joined her.

We archaeologists work together with local villagers who help us carefully dig, brush, scrape, sieve, wash and number all 'finds'. They also preserve the site. We tell them about the history of their village and they talk about it to visitors who come there. When they know how important the place is, they are proud to look after it.

A hut without a roof

"They are building a hut!" cried Selvam. "But it is inside the ground and has no roof."

"Stupid!" said Selvi. "It's not a hut. It's called a trench. Can't you see, they are digging out things buried in the earth. They will dig deeper and deeper every year and collect all they find. Then they will tell us stories about how people lived — ten thousand grandmothers ago!"

The team measured out a big square on the ground and bound it with ropes and pegs. Little ropes criss-crossed the big square. Within little boxes marked out on the old red earth, sat Selvi's father and some uncles. Each had a pickaxe and a brush and they were carefully clearing sand and silt and clay away from ancient stone tools.

A few centimetres at a time — dig-brush-dig. Sleepy old Uncle Chokkan swept the dug-out soil into little buckets and passed them on to Selvi's mother and aunts.

When we dig a trench we are actually digging through time — the deeper we dig, the older it gets. Like a stack of newspapers. If you start on 1st January and add one on top of the pile every day, by the end of the month 31st January will be right on top. It is the same with soil. So we have to dig very slowly, carefully peeling off layer by layer and recording what is found at each level.

Sometimes we dig for hours and hours and find nothing. It isn't much fun, in the hot sun. And then, excitement! A find! We carefully brush off the soil, measure its exact position, photograph it, draw it and record all details. Then we pack it in plastic bags and take it back to the camp to study further.

The women sat in their best saris in front of large sieves, bigger than the ones Selvi's mother used in the kitchen. They poured the soil into the sieve and picked out little shining stones and bits of bone and put them carefully in little plastic bags.

The city people were busy writing and measuring and drawing and photographing. They looked hot and tired, but happy. The heap of little plastic bags grew in size. Inside them — were they pieces of stone?

These 'rocks' are really handaxes. Just as the computer is perhaps the symbol of technology in our age, the Acheulian technology of *Homo erectus* is noted for the handaxe. As the picture shows, this was very beautifully made, shaped exactly the same on both sides. It was usually about 10-25 cm long, made of quartzite rock and would have had many uses – to dig for roots and tubers, kill and skin animals and so on. The design was so good that it lasted unchanged for thousands of years. Identical tools have been found in places far away from each other – in Africa, Europe and other parts of Asia.

"Stone? No!" thought Selvi. "Tools." Tools of ancient people in the river bed, over which she walked every day. Tools which every villager knew lay all over the red earth near the village. Everyone called them chakka-kal, 'shining stones', because they sparkled and shone in the sun.

"Come on, Grandfather," shouted an archaeologist. "Tell the children your stories of our work." Grandfather woke up from his sleep under a thorny bush and began . . . . .

The little box-like white marks on the trench floors that you can see in this and other photos are reference codes. These are slips on which the number of each 'find' is written. They help us record each artefact correctly, photograph it, draw it and then put it in a labelled bag. The white slips on the trench walls have numbers for the rows of squares on the floor, which help us mark the exact location of a find – just as in an atlas.

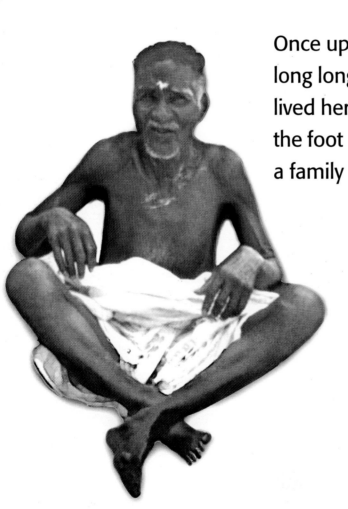

Once upon a time — this was a
long long time ago — there
lived here in this very land by
the foot of the Allikulli hills,
a family . . . . .

There was a little girl and a little boy and their parents, uncles, aunts and cousins. They lived thousands and thousands and thousands of years ago. The city people say they lived here 700,000 years ago. That's even older than Rama's time! More than 10,000 grandfathers ago!

There was a big river there, down near that dry gully. Today there's no water, but a long time back there was a big river and near the river there was a big lake.

Elephants and hippos and deer and buffaloes and birds came to the lake to drink water.

In the summer, the river dried up and the animals and birds crowded around tiny pools and waterholes.

In the monsoon, when the river waters flooded the land, they moved to the hills and plateaus.

This family of girl, boy, parents, uncles, aunts and cousins followed the ways of the animals.

In summer they camped close to the waterholes, and in the monsoon they lived in the little rock shelters and caves of the Allikulli hills . . . . .

Homo erectus means 'upright man'. This is what scholars called them though they were not the first species in the chain of evolution to stand upright. They lived from around 1.8 million to around 500,000 years ago. Most experts believe that they originated in Africa. They were hominins – that is, part of a family that includes all living humans and all their ancestors.

How did they look?
They were usually about 5-6 feet tall. But there is a fossil skeleton of a boy from Turkana in East Africa, aged 11 years or so, who was already around 5 feet tall! *Homo erectus* looked different from us – with a very prominent brow ridge over the eyes, jutting out face, broad nose, small chin and big teeth. And the brain was roughly two-third the size of ours.

Did they have families?
We don't know if they had families like we have today, but they lived in small groups and shared their food. From the locations of the tools we know that they camped where water, food and raw materials were easily available. They shared skills, which is how they developed such sophisticated tools.
To do things together they must have also communicated in some way with each other.

What was their life like?
We usually think of prehistoric communities as 'primitive', not 'developed' like us. But try living in a hostile landscape, with predators all around, unpredictable climates, a technology of only stone, bone and wood – and you will know how difficult it can be to just survive! *Homo erectus* survived, and did so very intelligently. They lived with great awareness of their environment, through some very major climatic changes – rising and falling sea levels, advancing and retreating masses of ice, and changes in animal and plant life. They migrated over much of Europe and Africa, and parts of Asia. They were efficient hunters and knew the use of fire. They ate mainly meat, along with roots, tubers and other plant food.

How long did they live?
Again, nothing is certain. But lifespans were very possibly short and 20 to 30 years would have been considered a 'ripe old age', as Grandfather says in his story.

She looks so strange!

"Did the little girl look like me?" asked Selvi.

"No," said Grandfather. "Look at the picture the archaeologists put up. That's what she looked like."

"Aiyo!" screamed Selvi. "She's short and hairy and has no chin. She has a huge forehead and big arms and legs. So do her parents. They look quite awful."

"She must have been a pretty girl for her time," said Grandfather. "Your father's not a film star either, is he, as I was in my days?"

"Come on, tell us more about the girl," the children shouted or else Grandfather would start on the old story of how he nearly made it in films.

The bearded archaeologist added: "Her people were our ancestors. We call them *Homo erectus*. Their bodies were much more powerful than ours and they had big teeth to be able to eat the kind of food they could find those days."

"I know *Homo erectus* and all the names," said Grandfather, irritated at being interrupted. "I also know that they were quite clever. The little girl and her family knew all about the plants and animals and insects and birds. They knew this land better than we do today — or nearly as well as I do."

"Above all they knew how to make tools of stone. Can you do that?" Grandfather asked and continued his story . . . . .

It was summer and very, very hot. The river had dried up. The little girl's family moved around small waterholes and looked for buried roots and tubers to eat. They were careful to keep away from the thirsty elephants and big buffaloes with huge horns.

The boys were out throwing sling balls at birds and rats and squirrels. The little girl sat on a rock watching her father. He had broken up a big boulder with Uncle's help and had a large piece of the flake on his lap. It was brown and shiny with sharp edges.

Father picked up a round smooth pebble from the river bed. He looked at the flake from all angles and then holding it on one knee, struck it sharply with the pebble. Bits of chips flew out in all directions. The little girl jumped out of the way.

Very carefully, he turned the flake in his hand and knocked off dozens of smaller pieces. Soon, a beautiful shape unfolded in his hands.

It was a handaxe — perfectly made and very, very sharp.

Father now picked up an old animal bone. He trimmed the edges of the tool in his hand and then sat back to examine it. The little girl jumped on his lap excitedly. She held the tool in her hands and admired it. It was better than what anyone else could have made. Her father was the best!

Father handed the tool to Mother who inspected it carefully and nodded. She had been busy making her own tools of wood, using stone and bone to scrape them into shape.

Next, Father and Uncle made dozens of tools from a large boulder. With new tools, the family was now ready to look for the day's meal. They spread out over the ancient river banks and found juicy tubers and roots buried within the clay. The handaxe and Mother's digging stick were perfect for digging them out and very soon a feast was in progress.

Suddenly, there was a thunderous noise near the river.

"Elephants! Elephants! They're coming, look! ". . . . .

The Archaeologists' Discovery

"Look!" Selvi, Selvam and Grandfather all jumped up as they heard the cry.

There was wild excitement in the trench. Two of the archaeologists were busy setting up cameras. Others shouted instructions. Aunts and uncles and mothers and fathers were hugging each other.

"Look here," cried the boss. "We've found footprints of animals, and handaxes and a tooth."

Selvi was disappointed. She thought they had found gold.

"Think of it," explained one of the archaeologists to the villagers crowding around. "Thousands of years ago, a baby animal ran across this clay and left behind its footprints. And the tooth is probably a child's, fallen here years and years ago."

Selvi peeped through into the trench. She could clearly see large round footprints in the soft clay. She could see the labels put down by the archaeologists, numbering each footprint. Wrapped in cotton was a tiny tooth, white but so big! It was broken in parts.

Scattered all over were big pointed tools they were calling handaxes. She began to get a little excited.

What if she too lost her tooth in the soil? Would it be found thousands of years later? Would her footprints near the river be preserved? What fun! She ran to ask Grandfather. But he wanted to finish the story . . . . .

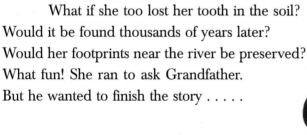

Footprints rarely survive. But at Laeotoli in Tanzania, Africa, they have. A group of Australopithecines (who lived even before *Homo erectus*) along with many other animals, birds and insects walked over a bed of soft wet volcanic ash. Soon after, the ash hardened, preserving a floor of footprints around 3 million years old! At Attirampakkam we found round marks in the clay, like the one circled in white in the photo below. Scholars say they are footprints of a Stone Age baby elephant. Next to it is a centimetre-scale, used to measure 'finds'.

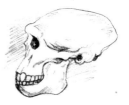 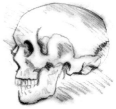

Most parts of the body decay, or are eaten by animals and birds as happened with hominids. But teeth are harder and more likely to survive. Which is lucky, for they give us vital clues – what species it belonged to, the food it ate, how old it was when it died and the environment it lived in. Compare a *Homo erectus* skull (left) with a modern human skull (right). Can you spot the differences?

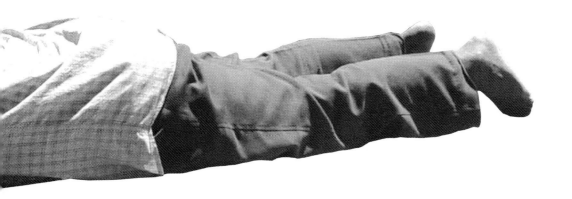

On that day there was no water in the river.
The elephants were very thirsty. A big herd had
gathered and was busily digging holes in the river
bed searching for water. Suddenly there was a
commotion.

A crocodile had caught hold of a baby
elephant's foot. The baby screamed in fright and its
mother and aunts dashed to its rescue. The crocodile
let go and the terrified baby elephant rushed out of
the pool, towards the girl's family.

'Run!' shouted the girl's father, and they sped
as fast as they could out of the way of the terrified
baby elephant and its family right behind it. The baby
dashed across the sticky clay and fled in the direction of
the little girl.

The girl was frozen in fear. Her father grabbed her in his
arms and pulled her out of the way, just in time. The herd
dashed past her. She could feel the earth shake. She could
smell them. Drops of muddy water sprayed all over her.
In a second they were gone. All that was left were footprints
in the clay.

Just then there was a thunderous roar in the skies.
Clouds rolled across from nowhere and drenched them in wild
bursts of rain. It was rain like the little girl had never seen
before. She and her family crowded under the spiky bushes as
the skies flashed with lightning.

Then the hills appeared to move. Torrents of water rushed down. The group dashed for higher land as they felt the earth shake beneath them. When they looked down they saw their little lake and clay beds covered by red earth and pebbles brought down from the hills.

There was no trace of Father's beautiful handaxes, and Mother's tools. The elephant footprints too had vanished, buried under red soil.

The storm was over in minutes. The family crept out and looked around. Pebbles lay everywhere — very good for making more stone tools. There were little streams flowing across the red earth.

Suddenly, the little girl felt blood trickling out of her mouth. Her tooth! In all the confusion, her tooth had fallen out. She ran her tongue across the big wide gap. Would she be able to eat again? Or would she look like old Grandma, who at the ripe old age of 20 had lost all her teeth?

A Party

That night there was a party at the site. The archaeologists were very happy and made long speeches in English. Selvi's father spoke in Tamil about the rich finds and the tools and the tooth.

Fathers and uncles ate and drank. Then they sang songs of Aiyyappa and Ankalamma and other gods and goddesses. One uncle made up a song about the finds in the trench and the archaeologists and sang it. Then they danced, slowly round and round in a circle.

There was chicken curry for all and rice and sambar and lots of sweets. The children sat in a row and ate hungrily. Selvi had eaten far too much and felt quite sleepy. Grandfather was softly singing a song about the past. He sang of a baby hippo stuck in the mud . . . . .

It was summer and there was no water. The baby was very weak. It sank down near the water and could not move again. The body lay close by the river's edge. The little girl's family saw it the next morning. Slowly they moved towards it. Hyenas and vultures were already hovering around it. The little group advanced more noisily now, throwing round stone balls and waste flakes to shoo away the animals and birds. Father and uncles quickly skinned the beast with their powerful scrapers. Then out came the choppers and handaxes. The bones were cut away from the flesh and the families carried away large chunks of meat. They smashed open the bones to get at the tasty marrow inside . . . . .

Grandfather sang of the tiny fire around which they roasted meat.

He sang of their great big teeth and powerful jaws smashing the bone to pieces.

He sang of the broken bones and tools which lay around for thousands of years after this feast.

He sang of the winds and the rain and clay and sands which covered them.

He sang of the villagers who found the bones.

He sang of the archaeologists who dug there and could tell the villagers about their culture, how old it was and what the rains used to be like thousands of years ago.

Selvi's Dream

One morning schoolchildren from the town came visiting. Cousin Jaychandran took them around. The big archaeologist called out to Selvi. "Come on. Tell the children all about the site." Selvi was very proud. She showed them the ancient tools. The children sat down and drew pictures of the trench and the tools. Selvi drew a big handaxe.

Stone tools, fossils of plants and bones, footprints – all these tell archaeologists what rocks were used for tools, how far people travelled to fetch good stone, what sort of plants and animals existed, climatic and geographical changes that took place, and more about the past.

Selvi had to see to it that the children did not pick up any tool or spoil the site.

Then the children went back to the town. Selvi was tired with all the excitement. Would she ever have such grand blue uniforms and smart ribbons, she wondered. Would she ever learn to write so well?

But right now there was important work to be done. The goats had wandered too close to the trench and one was chewing on a rope. Trouble!

The days passed quickly and it was time for the archaeologists to pack up. The trucks were loaded, goodbyes said, and payments made. All the workers got new clothes and a big bonus. There were smiles all around.

"Till next year then," the archaeologists shouted. "Guard the site. Don't allow anyone to pick up stone tools from the site. All this is yours. Look after it."

Selvi sat under a tree, dreaming. She dreamt that she was the little girl who had lived here in the past. These were her tools and her tooth that they had found. She handled the little handaxe the archaeologist had given her. She could clearly see her father giving it to her thousands of years ago.

Then it was the handaxe, now the computer, and what after this, Selvi wondered. She dreamt she had come back after a million years and saw . . .

"Wake up, stupid!" said Selvam. "Come, they have caught a snake down by the river. Let's go and see."

Mother was in the fields and father was sharpening his spade. The village was quiet. Grandfather was back in his cot under the neem tree waiting for the next dig. The children ran across the river to look at the snake. But Selvi could see someone standing on the site, half buried in red earth with a long wooden spear and handaxe. Or was that just the summer sun?

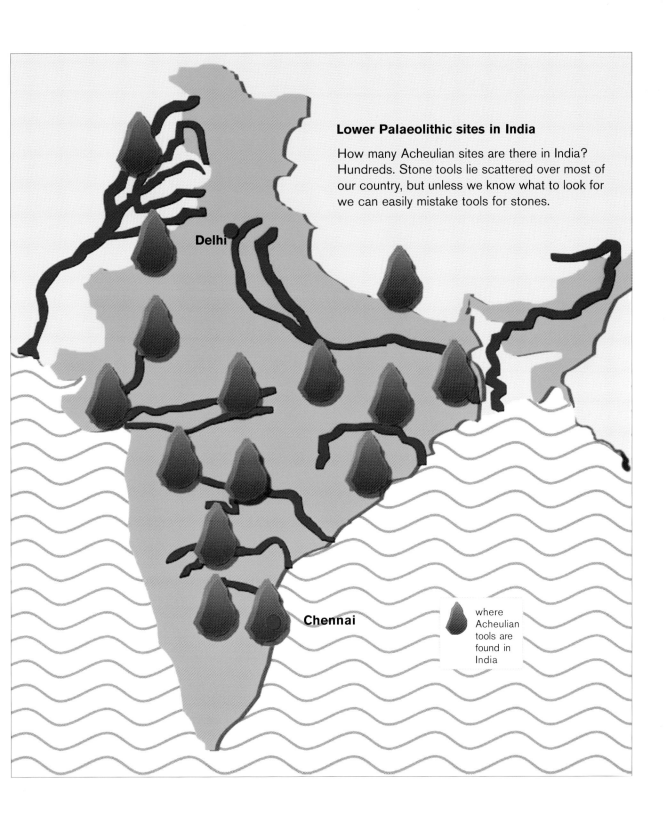

Lower Palaeolithic sites in India

How many Acheulian sites are there in India? Hundreds. Stone tools lie scattered over most of our country, but unless we know what to look for we can easily mistake tools for stones.

Delhi

Chennai

where Acheulian tools are found in India

The story of man

We can trace the origin of the 'modern human' to millions of years ago. But new discoveries being made almost every day keep changing the story of human evolution and how long ago our ancestors lived. So the time periods given in this very simple timeline are only approximate.

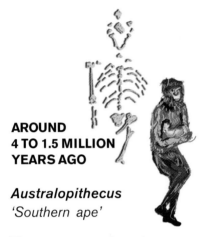

**AROUND
4 TO 1.5 MILLION
YEARS AGO**

Australopithecus
'Southern ape'

These are our earliest close relatives. Their fossils were discovered in Africa. The most famous one was of a female Australopithecine nicknamed 'Lucy' who lived in East Africa about 3 million years ago. The hip and thigh bones, knee joints and feet of these fossils show that this species walked upright. They were probably vegetarian, more hunted by wild animals than hunters themselves, and more like apes than humans.

**AROUND
2 TO 1.8 MILLION
YEARS AGO**

Homo habilis
'Handy man'

Fossils of a species distinct from Australopithecines were found in Olduvai Gorge in Africa by Louis Leakey. He named them *Homo habilis*, 'handy man' – because crude stone tools were also found here at the same archaeological level which showed that this species had started making things with their hands. He believed that they were our direct and most primitive ancestors, but more recent discoveries show that this may not be true.

**AROUND
1.8 MILLION TO
250,000 YEARS AGO**

Homo erectus
'Upright man'

The first fossils were found in Indonesia in the 19th century. By the 1940s, exciting fossil discoveries were made at Zhoukoudian in China, where they were called 'Peking Man'. More were found in Africa, the most famous of which is the 'Nariokotome boy' – he died at the age of 11 years and was around 5 ft tall, with long legs, and narrow hips and shoulders. They seem to have had larger brains than earlier hominins, knew the use of fire and made characteristic tools of the Lower Palaeolithic culture. They were probably the first hominin species to go 'Out of Africa'.

**AROUND
400,00 TO 200,000
YEARS AGO**

Archaic Homo sapiens
Older 'wise man'

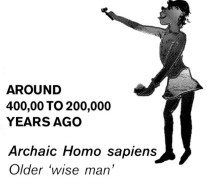

Most scholars believe that these early modern humans originated in Africa and then migrated elsewhere. By around 250,000 years ago, modern humans clearly appeared on the scene in Africa and migrated later to Eurasia. They are associated with tools of the Middle Stone Age or Middle Palaeolithic. This period follows the Lower Palaeolithic. In India, we have many sites of that time. They made tools like scrapers, borers and points with a technology called Levallois, which had a smarter way of using raw material.

**AROUND
200,00 TO 30,000
YEARS AGO**

*Homo sapiens
Neanderthalensis*

Discovered first in the Neander valley in Germany, they lived in Europe and western Asia. They had large brains, short stocky bodies and large broad noses, and were mainly adapted to withstand the cold climates of the last Ice Age in Europe. They made stone tools of the Middle Palaeolithic phase. They also buried their dead. About 25,000 years ago, they eventually became extinct, perhaps because of climatic changes or severe competition with the Cro-Magnons – the newly emerging anatomically modern humans. They never lived in India.

**AROUND
50,000 YEARS AGO
TILL TODAY**

Homo sapiens sapiens
Modern 'wise man'

The origins of modern humans similar to ourselves, lie in Africa around 100,000 years ago. Studies of ancient DNA tell us that by 50,000 years ago, fully modern humans lived in Africa, from where they slowly spread all over the world. In Europe they are called Cro Magnons. They are associated with the Upper Palaeolithic culture or Late Stone Age. They made sophisticated stone tools called blades. They also engraved bone and ivory and painted rock shelters. In India, we find many sites with blade tools and ostrich eggshell beads.

What next?

FROM STONE AGE TO CYBER AGE

the handaxe . . . to an archaeologist's tools today

compass for finding directions

laptop computer for entering and analysing data

range of brushes for brushing away soil

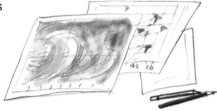

satellite image which shows what the site looks like from space, and graph-sheets and pencils for drawing

measuring tape and scales for measuring

cameras

conservation box with chemicals and other material to conserve delicate finds.

Total Station laser theodolite for mapping

pens, pins, clips, sample collection bags, pens and tags to mark tools

trowels and knives for carefully exposing tools

dentist's fine tools for digging delicate finds

white 'pottery' bags for final packing and transport

notebooks for recording information